DEATH ROW
ROW ROW
YOUR BOAT

KURT LUCHS

Sagging
Meniscus

© 2024 by Kurt Luchs

All Rights Reserved.

Set in Mrs Eaves XL with LaTeX.

ISBN: 978-1-952386-98-5 (paperback)
Library of Congress Control Number: 2024937178

Sagging Meniscus Press
Montclair, New Jersey
saggingmeniscus.com

To Elizabeth

We are such stuff
As dreams are made on, and our little life
Is rounded with a sleep.

—William Shakespeare, *The Tempest*, Act IV Scene 1

Contents

I. Night Thoughts & Death Songs

II. Other Lives, Other Endings

III. Mortal Loves, Tribes, Families

DEATH ROW ROW ROW YOUR BOAT

I.

Night Thoughts

&

Death Songs

A Mist in the Tree

Every cell in my body has been replaced
many times, my books tell me,
until not one atom remains
of the original me
and this simulacrum in my shape
may contain molecules that once
belonged to Jesus or Hitler or Homer
or W. C. Fields.
I'd like that—I mean,
if it were W. C. Fields.
Neither this fading map to nowhere
we call memory
nor this firefly lost in the Grand Canyon
we call consciousness
can tell us anything useful,
we've been set adrift without oars or compass,
but despite the endless duplications
something singular persists,
something that thinks it has a right
to speak with a capital "I,"
something that thinks it thinks
though scarcely ever finishing a thought.
If this half-withered tree
rooted in the earth and slowly
bending to return to it
is my life
then I am a mist in the tree,
in it and of it and indivisible from it
yet also somehow apart from it.
Many say they know
what happens to the mist when the tree dies,
but this question has always
been above my pay grade,
and anyway it's so foggy
I can't see a thing.

Mine

At night everything belongs to me,
the deserted streets, the lights
blinking out a code that only I can decipher,
the rain a curtain rung down again and again
on a play that never quite opened,
written by and starring yours truly,
silent partner of the nocturnal.
Yes, at night it's all mine,
and in the best possible way:
ownership without responsibility,
like the commissar of a hydroelectric dam
deep in the Urals. It's my dam,
of course it is, but it's also
the people's dam, and when it breaks
the people will pay for it.
The people always pay.
Fortunately the night doesn't break much
except for a few hearts.
Mine was broken long ago.
The night did it, and the rain, and the lights
that know nothing, illuminate nothing,
blinking like stuttering imbeciles,
and I am a cup bearing the rain,
brimming over with the night,
a leaking cup with a chip and a crack
that can still be smashed for no reason
on the sidewalk that belongs to me.

A Brief Word About the Moon

She's moving away from us
a few inches every year,
the longest breakup in history,
and perhaps by the time
she's free of our gravity
we won't even be here
to mark the occasion, moving
on ourselves through stranger pastures
beyond this brief and precious
thing called life to lands
unknown and unknowable, the final
mystery after love has left
and what will it matter
then without her quicksilver face
to shine down upon us?

A Song of Starlight

Some unknown poet from the Greek Anthology
lies on his or her back looking at the stars,
and I am right there with them
in the middle of the Mediterranean night
staring unblinking at the blinking Pleiades,
nearly the same after all these years
because two millennia in the life of a star
is but the blink of a cosmic eye.
Whatever else has changed we still share this
sense of beauty and wonder at the night sky,
and the illusion that because it evolves so slowly
it is permanent, fixed. In truth,
nothing is permanent, nothing is fixed.
And yet stars long dead send us their light,
ancient photons penetrating our eyes,
kissing our skin, and the words of singers
also dead many years touch us in the same way,
the words still alive in another language
though the names of the poets are forgotten.
And perhaps the songs are more beautiful
because we don't know who sang them.

"Where Do We Come From? What Are We? Where Are We Going?"

(Title and inscription of a painting by Paul Gauguin.)

Always the big questions
from the troubled post-Impressionists.
Well, Paul, now that you mention it,
I come from a long line of genetic mutants
whose total dysfunction is somehow
greater than the sum of its individual sadnesses.
It's a miracle any of us could master the basics
of reproduction and manage to pass on
our defective inheritance.
What I am is a piece
of dying meat that seems to think
it has time to ponder its own mortality
and the meaning—if any—of existence.
So we have that in common at least.
Where we are going is a tricky one,
seeing as there is no "we," nor am I
about to set foot in Tahiti,
and if I did, no masterpieces would emerge
because I am not an artistic genius
despite leaving my own wife behind in another world.
Still, I love your questions,
which mystify and haunt me even more
than your dark tropical canvasses.
Where are you?

Homunculus

Oracle or pincushion, which did they intend
who fashioned him from a single reed
and a whitening lock of human hair?

The mouth a vicious daub of red,
partially healed and not meant
for speech.

The ears still green;
buds, perhaps, opening for a syllable
yet to be named,

a hissing song. Whatever it is
the tiny fists have closed on,
they aren't letting go.

The feet mere stubs fit not even for planting.
At his side the painted blade hangs blue and ready.
What color the eyes, rolled inward forever?

Coffee

The only approved addiction in the land
of working till you drop, it's a cup of life,
no matter how bitter we always want more,
cream and sugar, real or not, cannot quite quell
the taste of darkness that drags us into light
kicking and screaming inwardly as our heart
accepts the imitation adrenaline
and the fight or flight response triggered thereby,
nothing to fight but sleep, nowhere to fly but
deeper into the day's minutia, awake
in body and mind alone, the soul still lost
in the waves of Lethe, not to be restored
to mindfulness of itself by anything
so trivial as the hot kiss of caffeine.

Socrates

Almost every dialogue follows the same pattern.
Socrates is talking to a businessman,
or a soldier, or a politician, or one of the idle rich
who has time for these word games.
All he does is ask questions.
Seemingly innocent questions, like a detective
with the endless patience of the police laying a trap:
What is virtue? Why are we here?
Is there a righteous form of government?
Whatever the topic, the poor fellow starts
by confidently mouthing the current platitudes
but Socrates will have none of it.
Question follows question with the ruthless precision of chess
until every comforting illusion has been stripped away,
every pretense of knowledge, and the other person in the dialogue
has been shown to be as ignorant as the day he was born.
The reader can be pardoned for concluding
Socrates is an asshole, just as the Greek rulers did.
I used to think that. Now I think
he's the kindest person who ever lived.
Life is so precarious, so short.
We enter it with nothing, we leave the same way.
We cannot improve on the poverty of existence
except with wisdom, and there is no room for wisdom
in a mind that thinks it already knows something.
These days I find I have been permanently infected
with the philosopher's questions, I cheer him on
in every dialogue, and as he raises his glass
of hemlock, I raise mine too,
the house serving no other beverage, and I discover peace
in admitting I know nothing, I never did.

Apology

May I speak freely?
Thank you. That makes it easier.
How disappointed you must be,
sitting there expecting something more,
an insight or two, a scrap of wisdom,
a bit of beauty dressed up in rhyme
or alliteration or the dazzling lies of metaphor.
Unfortunately, this is all I have for you.
We woke up in the same unfurnished apartment
chained to the same radiator
by the same absentee landlord
who has never once shown his face.
Occasionally food and drink appear,
occasionally a bucket.
When we tire of screaming our fool heads off
there follows the delightful contrast of silence
which always feels as if
it's about to say something, but never does.
And that is a statement in itself I suppose.
Why do we scream?
He's been getting away with it for billions of years.
There is no chance of him
being brought to justice anytime soon.
The changing seasons, the few square inches
of sky and cloud we can see through the window
leave you mute but make me want to sing.
It takes all kinds to make a world,
even such a world as this.
If only my song brought comfort to one of us,
like the shadow of the tree
that crosses the wall each day,
slowly lengthening, almost as if
the tree were growing, almost
as if it were really there.
Perhaps it is. Most likely we'll never know.
We lie down with illusion
and wake up with mystery,
born in chains, dying in chains,
my song the only thing that ever escapes,
that can come and go as it pleases.
I'm so sorry.

A Real Question with No Real Answers

What is hope?
A moss that grows
silent and unseen
on any surface,
a light that becomes visible
only after your eyes
have adjusted to the darkness,
a note that hangs in the air
after the bird has flown,
a green shoot erupting
from a dead stump.

Sworn enemy of reason,
dubious friend of life,
estranged cousin of death,
confounder of statistics,
historians and tax collectors.

When you talk to yourself
she's listening,
without a word
but holding your hand
and gazing over your shoulder
at a future
that might still be.

She sees what has not
quite come to pass
and perhaps never will,
the path un-walked,
and yet—this is confusing—
she remains blind and deaf
to whatever would be
unhelpful to perceive,
her every affirmation
contains a denial.

She scratches the face
of disaster and carries
a mustard seed
under one fingernail.

Psalm

Make a joyful noise
unto the wallpaper,
let us sing unto the ice pick,
unto the man who squints
in the presence of the light.

Dear Lord, it's me!
The light is drilling a pinhole
through my head
for the angels to take aim at that pool
of grease, my life.

Someone's loving hands
pressed to my temples,
prophetic phosphenes
offering a preview
of tonight's coming attractions.

I am useless and dangerous,
or perhaps merely useless.
Why then do I wake
with blood on my fingers,
meat in the refrigerator

and a clean conscience?
From every face, in every eye
my narrow grave yawns,
bored with the prospect
of admitting me.

Do You Know These 10 Common Warning Signs of Depression?

Not able to get out of bed
because you are handcuffed to a 1200-pound Kodiak bear
that has four tranquilizer darts in its neck and snores.

Persistent thoughts of harming yourself
by eating at Taco Bell.

Little everyday things that used to bring you joy,
like setting fire to your city and throwing bricks in policemen's faces,
now seem more like work than play.

Pieces of darkness flake off of night's canopy
to settle on you slowly, gently, until
you are covered in a uniform layer of black ash.

You suddenly realize you are rooting for the administrative assistant
in the Lifetime Original Movie you're watching,
the energetic young woman who wants to seduce the husband,
kidnap the child and murder the wife.

Even the voices in your head
don't want to talk to you anymore.

When sleep finally comes there are no dreams,
merely an announcer saying that that service
is only available to Premium Subscribers.

You find yourself pretending that every bill that drops
through your mail slot is a letter from a dear friend
threatening you with violence unless you repay the money you borrowed.

Loss of appetite except for truffles; apparently even a very sad person
can eat an entire box of those.

A small bronze plate appears mysteriously
on your bedroom door to declare that occupancy
by more than one person is both unlawful and ludicrous.

No Reason

This morning for no reason at all
joy wells up inside me,
joy beams from my eyes
and radiates from my fingertips,
everything blesses me
and I bless everything in turn
like a lazy savior signing heavenly invoices
without even reading them.
It's a kind of madness, friend,
because I have money troubles,
I have family troubles the same as you
and planet Earth has human troubles
as on any day the sun rises.
Joy must come from one of those
hidden dimensions the scientists
are always yammering about,
a compactified place
filled with compressed infinities
that leave no room for ordinary misery.
When an impossibly minute piece of joy
leaks out, it transforms
the nearest being for what seems
an eternal moment.
This morning, for no reason at all,
that being is me.

False Spring

We know it can't last.
It's still February, and it always snows in March
and April, and sometimes even in May.
We'll take it though, the hunks of ice
shrinking and sliding off the roof
into puddles that weren't there yesterday,
the rivulets from melting snow almost as loud
as a rainstorm, coming off of everything
under the bright turquoise horizon.
I level entire towns of slush with Gene Kelly kicks
while whistling show tunes from musicals
that haven't been written yet,
I dare the craven cold to show its pinched little face
one more time, knowing it will tomorrow,
when all this will be as if it had never been.
The hell with tomorrow.
Today it's spring, all day, as free as the sky
but only one per customer, thank you so very much.
I close my eyes and pretend it's raining.

Nonbeing

Now, I am.
Soon, I will not be.
I've spent my whole life
scrabbling just to live

even as death was growing in me
like the bee's honeycomb.
I'm late to the wake
and I bring nothing to it

but wide-eyed wonder,
yet still, with the philosophers
and mystics, I find sweetness
in seeking to know

the mystery of nonexistence,
the secret of nonbeing,
such a vastness compared
to my brief time on earth.

Will it be an unraveling,
a dissolving into nothingness,
or an entwining into everything
minus the personal?

From here it appears
the personal is all there is,
all that matters anyway.
Some say death is part of life.

I say life is part of death;
death is so much bigger
and lasts so much longer.
I'd surrender my sword to it

except that the sword
was never mine and I was born
with it dangling over me
by a single invisible thread.

Death Row

The newspaper gets smaller every year.
Soon it will be a postcard
with a tinted photo
of the city on one side
and obituaries on the other.

Speaking of death, I see she came
for Charlie last night,
cutting off his wind as effectively
as holding a pillow over his face.
It says here the official cause

was pneumonia, drowning
in his inner lagoon,
but I think we can chalk that up
to a failure of investigative journalism.
We're all on death row.

It's just a matter of time
and there will be
no last-minute reprieves.
Most nights I fall asleep
with a book propped against a pillow

and the flashlight on,
forgetting to mark my place
with that lovely postcard
which may or may not have
my name on the other side.

First and Last

The first rays of dawn shot slantwise
through the blinds. I stirred
and rolled over to face death
staring at me in her quiet way
which I have come to admire.
A clumsier companion would have blurted out,
"I love to watch you sleep,"
but with us there is no need for words.
I have no idea what she is thinking
and that is the beauty of it.
Love requires mystery and surrender.
Between us we have both.
When the unheralded moment arrives
my capitulation will be unilateral
and her conquest of my being complete.
Then I will know, if I have time to reflect,
whether her final gift is a bullet,
a head-on collision in the night,
or the slow, halting waltz of neurological decay.
For now we sip coffee from the same cup,
as close as two creatures can be,
watching the sunrise together,
and only one of us knows
whether it's the last.

Breakfast with Death

I stick with the classics—
two eggs, bacon, English muffin—
while she orders a giant cinnamon roll.
"Why should I worry about calories
and refined sugar?" she laughs.
But then she's never in a bad mood,
things always seem
to work out for her somehow.
She's the first one to read my verses.
"That's not quite there, is it?" she'll say,
crinkling her nose and adding,
"Don't worry, time fixes everything."
"I wouldn't know," I say,
"I'm not dating time, I'm dating you."
Then she laughs that incomparable laugh,
like the first church bell of the morning,
and I fall in love with her all over again.
How long, I wonder, before the cholesterol
in the eggs, the fat in the bacon
or the processed flour in the English muffin
help her put me in the ground?

My Dream

The simple, honest people of my little town
form a circle and put me in the middle of it.
They begin to pelt me with copies
of *The Lottery and Other Stories* by Shirley Jackson,
first the paperback, which gives me minor welts and bruises
and yes, paper cuts, and then the hardcover,
which does more serious damage,
breaking my nose, taking out one eye,
then the other, causing a concussion
and eventually both a heart attack and a stroke.
As I lay dying, with a completely unintentional
and irrelevant Faulkner reference,
I thought I heard a mother scold a child
for accidentally throwing a copy
of *The Haunting of Hill House*. Or was that
a dream within the dream?
No matter. I was happy to have been a live human
for a few decades, and even happier now
to be a dead metaphor.

The Rains of October

The rains of October lay a cold, damp hand
between your shoulder blades, they say to every fallen leaf
stop blowing around, stay down, be still, decay.
They mark the ends of things, these rains,
and they say to the rest of us
death need not hurt, or if it does then pain
is needful, death is good, death is right,
enjoy us for what we are while you can
for all too soon another change will come
and there will be only the sweet amnesia of snow.
Heed the rains, the ice is coming, the ice is coming
the planet whispers as she whirls alone in space.

Meditation

The long shuddering intake of breath
From the air conditioner
Plays its one plaintive note
For all it's worth
So much feeling in that undying
Death rattle
I believe more than the air
Is being conditioned
And behind it the cry of crickets
Where there are no crickets
The crickets are in me
All of this is somewhere in me
And I am somewhere else
A vista opening upon a verge
Scenes waiting to become sounds
Sounds waiting to become words
Words waiting to become thoughts
Thoughts waiting to remake the world
Because the world they behold
Is unbearably bright and utterly silent
Strange and beautiful and terrifying

Ode to Silence

I've never heard you, if I'm being honest.
For many years now a mild case of tinnitus
has left me with the continual chirp of locusts
or crickets in my ears, not unpleasant,
actually a sort of comfort, but it does mean
there is always a noise in my head. Before that
I don't recall ever experiencing complete quiet
even for a moment.
There was the hum of the air conditioner
the cough of the furnace
the breeze rustling the blinds
distant thunder or the low rumble of traffic
the neighbor's dog barking at the end of his chain
a tomcat howling for sex
music from the house on one side
and television from the house on the other.
If nothing else, the sigh of my own breathing
the beat of my heart counting down my life.
And now we're getting to it, silence.
I've never heard you, yet I wonder
if I will at the end, or right after
and if so will you be
a period at the end of the sentence
or an ellipsis marching ever forward
into the blankness of the page?

Listening to Arvo Pärt's *Tabula Rasa*

I. Ludus: With Movement

I'm sorry to tell you, purists and poseurs,
intellectual snobs, that music is no mere abstraction,
it has content, it tells a story, and any fool can follow it.
Here we have a soul in torment, the default human condition,
and if you doubt the soul's existence you still need to explain
what it is that writhes in agony, a caged creature
seeking to escape, throwing itself again and again
against the wall of reality. Some might call it
a glandular imbalance. I call it a spiritual crisis
of no particular origin, though one is tempted to hear in it
echoes of the composer's longing to leave the iron embrace
of the Soviet Union, something he managed a few years
after writing this. The commissars of culture
didn't like his serialism (as it turned out later,
he didn't much care for it himself), and when
he started creating overtly religious works, they did him
the great reverse honor of making him a nonperson,
a phenomenon that is so much fun it has finally
reached our shores and been embraced by the West.

In 1977 when he wrote this, however, his body was still
trapped and his spirit was only beginning to soar above
his early twelve-tone style, a chrysalis happily abandoned.
In any spiritual struggle, suffering comes first, understanding later.
Blind, mute pain precedes almost every visionary song.

So it is here, in the movement "With Movement,"
a nondescript way to describe ten minutes of exquisite thrashing
that seems to recapitulate the history of the 20th century
while recalling such fellow Eastern Bloc cellmates
as Bartok and Penderecki and even a bit
of Bernard Herrmann in the shower scene from *Psycho*.
Yet all things have an end, and just when we think
we can't take any more, the movement "With Movement"
stops moving, stops stabbing. Blessed silence.
Everyone breathes—performers, audience, perhaps even
the instruments themselves. And then . . .

II. Silentium: Without Movement

The title of the second movement misleads, but only slightly.
If not exactly silence, there is a profound quietude,
and if not precisely still, there is merely the barest movement,
a kneeling shadow doing the impossible, trying to crawl
into the light. The crisis has passed. Has the pain passed as well?

No. It has assumed another form, a hollow, a cistern,
filling drop by drop with grief. With each falling sigh of the strings
the soul brims over once more. And we thought it was love
that was unending. How many tears can be pressed
from the lonely grape of humanity? And must the grape drink
its own vintage? We could refuse to drink, we have the right
to refuse, that's what makes us human after all, and not
fleshy robots. But no: we will drink. It's all we have in the end.
Happiness comes and goes, amusement, passion, industry,
all the modes of anesthesia, are cactus flowers that open and close
in one day. Only grief is eternal, say the descending strings,
back and forth, lower each time, seeking the ground of being,
until at last they find acceptance, surrender, peace.

This is the movement that patients in hospice ask to hear
while they prepare to float quietly out of this existence,
the strings vibrate in tune with the filaments of their souls
as they start to fray and unfurl into the void. This movement
speaks to the dying of suffering endured and transfigured,
of the spirit honed on the knife-edge of sorrow to a kind of purity,
which leaves it no longer at home in this world,
ready for the next, if there is one, but at any rate
finally girded to say a final goodbye. And when the end comes
we hardly recognize it, so slight the slipping away, so gentle
the last little wave carrying us into the unknown.

The Woman in the Mirror

The dead are dead, when they're gone they're gone,
they cannot return. Except sometimes they do.
Tonight as I was dining with my darling
in our favorite restaurant, I looked up

to see the sweet narrow face of a woman long dead
staring back at me obliquely from the side mirror
on the wall: Andrea Nagy Smith,
not seen on earth since 2012,

dear friend, lover of cats and jokes,
honorary aunt to my two daughters,
how is it you are here this evening
a bit younger than when we first met

in New Haven? Who is this man with you?
Where is the husband you found late in life
after so much time alone, the one
who gave you such brief, intense joy?

What realm have you returned from
and what message do you bring me
other than an overpowering urge to weep?
I don't know, I don't know, but I see now

you've been alive inside me all this time
as well as in the mirror world
and possibly also in this world
which I could have sworn you had left.

All of My Fathers

(for Robert Bly, 1926–2021)

All of my fathers are dead now.
If I have any further questions
there is no one to ask, no one
whose answer might matter to me.
But then it was you who taught me

that the deader a father is, the more
he lives inside us, and the more urgent
it becomes to build a room for him
in the house of the psyche,
lest we be ruled unknowingly by a monster

chained and howling in the basement
or a madman hiding in the attic,
eating dead spiders and dust.
Thanks to you, I built such a room
for my earthly father, and so reclaimed

the life and light and joy
he had stolen from his seven children.
Only then was I able to follow you
and all of my real fathers
through the open door in the soul

to the beauty of the word.
From you I also learned that the good father
contains a mother made of earth
and air and fire and water,
but that's a story for another day,

perhaps another life. Right now I need
to revisit the room I built for you,
the one lined with books and lit
by a single round window facing the sun
and looking out on new snow and silence.

A Last Villanelle

(for Brett Foster, 1973–2015)

The best beauty is of things as they go.
I sing the fading sigh, the falling leaf.
Beauty passes, and passing makes it so.

I celebrate the loss of all I know,
The sure opinion and unsure belief.
The best beauty is of things as they go.

I watch things die where some would watch them grow.
Glory comes with whatever comes to grief.
Beauty passes, and passing makes it so.

So much better the arrow than the bow,
And better the mad flight, however brief.
The best beauty is of things as they go.

No sight compares with the sun sinking low,
Turning waves gold as they break on the reef.
Beauty passes, and passing makes it so.

I seek the final fire, the final snow.
Finality itself is my motif.
The best beauty is of things as they go.
Beauty passes, and passing makes it so.

Sudden Silence

(for Adam Zagajewski, 1945–2021)

A certain music has stopped.
As when the voice of a bird
calling from a lone tree
grows suddenly silent
the moment you draw near.
We won't have that tune again
except in books, where music goes to die
or sometimes to live.
I think yours will live
after a hush in the pine forest
and a pause and many tears.

A certain music has stopped.
A music notable for daring to be uncertain
during an age of official certitudes
when any question, however tentative,
was a political act.
In this as in a multitude of things
you were the father I would have preferred,
the older brother I never had,
the professor whose master class I did not take
but from which I learned anyway, stealing whatever I could.

A certain music has stopped.
You grew up amid rubble both physical and metaphysical,
which must be how you learned that a broken thing
can still be beautiful, like the human spirit
or the collapsing cathedral we call civilization.
For me and countless others
you became the reluctant choir leader
stubbornly continuing to sing in the ruins.

A certain music has stopped.
And perhaps now would be the time
to remember that music is also
the space between the notes,
the little silences that give meaning
to the greater silence,
the music that does not stop.

Around the Block

(for Charles Simic, 1938–2023)

No more strolling down dark city streets.
No more pausing to look into resale shop windows
astonished at what people have owned
and what they have surrendered.
No more trying to decipher

the cries of crows in bare winter trees
or the trees themselves, their branches twisted
with the secret arthritis of old plants.
The world, though infinitely opaque
and puzzling, is not a puzzle to be solved

or a body to be dissected
but a mystery to be embraced
like the lovely Helen when you return
from your walk and leave your shoes
on the mat for the last time.

Fog and Fire

Fog lay on the land like gauze
on a wound that wouldn't heal,
holding the sickness close
to keep s scab from forming.
Or at least that's how it seemed to me.
I'm often a bit depressed
before my first cup of coffee.
I was busy keeping my morbid thoughts to myself
when Mrs. Sheldon emerged from the mist
completely covered in flames.
The most terrifying part was that
she wasn't screaming. Apart from burning
from head to foot she was her normal self.
She smiled as she passed, said "Good morning!"
and disappeared back into the fog.
A few seconds later Jake Louis came along
the same path, carrying his beach sandals
and also blazing away while feeling no pain.
He grunted, which is about all
you'll ever get out of Jake, but not because
his swimming trunks were nearly burned off,
he didn't appear to notice that,
scorched and smoldering though he was.
I stopped right there and sat down
on a sand dune, pondering these portents.
Not half a minute had gone by
when the Nisbett sisters burst upon the scene,
all four of them, flames shooting out of them
every which way. They were giggling and waving.
I waved back and realized my own arm
was on fire and I couldn't feel a thing.
It's one thing to come upon an apocalypse.
It's quite another to take part.
I stood up, turned toward Lake Michigan
and began walking into the waves, wondering
which primal element would consume me first.
The fog was finally beginning to lift.

The Two Lights

Something about the way the human lights come on
at this point in the evening, how the first
of their glow shines against the last
of the natural light, our neon brightness growing
as the sun diminishes and the sky's fierce colors
fade from red and orange into pale blue and the clouds
become bits of purple-gray seaweed swept back
under the wave of dark which is the horizon
and the night washes over us and the stars
remain, sparkling pebbles on a beach
that stretches farther than we can see.

II.

Other Lives,
Other Endings

Tabula Rasa

As usual, I was struggling
to find a few well-chosen words
that might reveal the music
of the mundane, the song
the world hums under its breath
that could begin to make
sense of it all.
As usual, I failed.
I thought I heard the hum
swell, draw near and stop,
then moments later felt
the tiny sting of the mosquito
on my forehead as it drank
a drop of my brain blood.
My hand moved faster
than my mind or the mosquito,
splashing my blood and her body
on the blank page,
and what it wrote
was for my eyes only.

Spider

My ceiling her floor,
the very concept of ceiling absent
from her world.

She has somewhere to get to
in a hurry,
and the faster

her silent legs move
the more my heart races,
keeping time.

Such purpose
one only sees in salesmen
and murderers.

My broom a vengeful
god overshadowing
her many wide eyes.

Encounter

In the fine white gravel at my feet
something quick, alive, disturbing the dust . . .
It stops in my shadow—
a five-legged wolf spider.
Two legs are simply missing
while another drags brokenly behind.
We watch each other on the quiet road.
The breeze ruffles the tiny hairs on his back.
I'd like to think my soul great enough
to encompass a crippled spider
but I see nothing between us,
nothing. Half-hobbling
he's made it alone this far,
and at the approach of a curious fingertip
he's gone.

Secret Messages

Life is a record album I sometimes listen to backward
searching for secret messages,
though the ones I hear playing it forward the usual way
are no less mysterious.
Just now, for example, I notice a spider
has claimed a corner of the ceiling
where three straight lines converge
as in a painting by Mondrian,
only at the center of this composition is murder
if you happen to be a fly or a moth.
Does death really have to be in the middle of a thing
before we can call it beautiful?
Earlier today I was listening to Simon and Garfunkel
singing "Save the Life of My Child,"
a song I've known all my life, about a boy leaping
to his doom from a New York building,
and for the first time I heard the words
"Hello darkness my old friend"
inserted from an older song, slowed down
and buried in the mix so as to be almost unrecognizable.
Yet there it was, a secret message hiding in plain sight,
waiting all these years for me to finally pay attention.

"I long to enter the unholy . . ."

I long to enter the unholy
veins of lightning
like the sound of breaking glass,
to trace the shudder that
flashes through clouds and shakes
the dead in their new shoes;
to lie down in the soft coffins of long grass
as in a woman's thighs,
and never breathe again
unless my breathing were the wind.

I long to fall forever
between stars, into the dark
like a hole someone is still digging;
to burrow in the drifts of snow like silence;
to be the shadow that walks away
when a man dies.

Tree

What does it mean to be
planted in one patch of soil
for your entire existence?
To stand there forever
because your lone leg
can't go anywhere.
The struggle for survival
no less bitter, overshadowed
by this one's leaves,
out-drunk by that one's roots.
An orchestra of bark flutes
played by each passing wind.
The winds which one day
will lay you out
among the corpses of your kind
to slowly become the loam
in which you were born.
There is a sort of horror
to it all, so much beauty too,
reaching for sky and sun
like you really mean it.
Putting the rest of us to shame
who walk where we will
heads down, looking into the earth
and seeing nothing
for what it is.

Two Sisters

Dingo is the smart one
But Wombat has the looks
In the family, a dark

Tortoiseshell with limbs
That seem cut from soft stone
And eyes deep as a green and black sea.

Age and arthritis have made her
Walk like an old Chinese woman
Carrying a bundle of sticks.

At rest though—which is twenty-three
Hours out of twenty-four—
She's the loveliest thing that ever lived.

You can't help but feel the Egyptians
Were half-right to worship them,
These creatures that own us and deign

To let us attend upon them
With our inferior offerings
Of processed fish and turkey.

We are not worthy!
Dingo has somehow divined the horrible
Secrets of the human calendar.

She knows a visit to the vet
Is nigh and hides under the bed
Howling as if her

Last kitten had been drowned.
Wombat remains ignorant and serene.
Which sister is the wiser?

To honor the feline demiurge I have
Given up reading the newspaper (no great
Loss, let's be honest)

And will devote my remaining days
To absorbing the warmth of the
One true god, the sun, that giant cat's eye.

The Dog One Floor Up

He begins howling the minute she leaves,
long before sunrise, dressed in pastel blue scrubs,
and he seldom pauses until she returns,
though sometimes the howl subsides into a sob
or a quiet moan. You would think someone
was working him over with molten fire tongs
but it's merely the leading cause of death, loneliness,
and in this we are all mammals together.
While he howls outwardly, I do it inwardly,
my cries echoing down empty corridors somewhere
inside me, audible only to myself. In my case
no one is coming back, so the inner howl
continues nonstop, like tinnitus or a fire alarm,
until it becomes a kind of companion,
one I would almost miss if it were gone
and at whose sudden absence I might well
begin howling out loud in unison with
that poor creature I have never even seen
in the apartment one floor above me.

Coyote

I thought it was the electric fan whining
until it climbed up an octave
and trilled in that way they have,
defiant and forlorn and exhilarated
all at the same time.
That snapped me awake and to attention.
The purple sky was dark, overcast, no moon
behind the clouds, but the fireflies
sent flashes through the meadow,
brief, blurry halos of illumination
like a medieval engraving inked in
with color by a much later monk.
There was something else under the howling
and the wind tossing the trees,
and when the coyote pounced
in the tall grass and brought its jaws down
I knew it was a rabbit.
The death cry went up,
a sound you never forget,
not unlike soldiers crying for their mothers
in their final moments, and then
it was all over but the chewing
and one last little howl, this time of triumph.
I lay back, unable to fall asleep again
for a while. When I did, I dreamed
I was on all fours in the open field
loping toward the long dark grass,
looking for my pack.

Ode to the Swamp

We compare Washington, DC, to you
as if that's an insult, and it is,
but not the one intended.
Our nation's capital is the home office of death
whereas you contain life without measure.
In fact, something very much like you
may well have been the birthplace of life,
a soup of organic compounds, carbon dioxide, methane,
the first amino acids and who knows what else
brought to earth by ice-bearing asteroids and comets
and gradually gaining in complexity until
lightning strikes, the sun works its mysteries
and all at once self-organization occurs,
there is a cell wall and within it
the original individual, one ready to become two.
Billions of years later the results of this cosmic experiment
sit quietly gazing at each other without fear
though some are predators, some prey,
and this one, more bloodthirsty than any other species,
is today merely an observer. I see the head of a baby
snapping turtle poking out of your murky waters
pretending to be a twig near your shore,
if a swamp even has a shore.
The grasshoppers, master cellists of the insect realm,
are making music with their legs.
Once again the red-winged blackbirds play the part
of brightly uniformed doormen barring entry
to an exclusive dwelling, hurling abuse
from their bobbing cattail territories,
the most obstreperous and aggressive of songbirds.
I move to stretch a cramp out of my leg
and a leopard frog that had been hidden
leaps back into you with a squeak,
returning to the source in a way,
and I am tempted to follow her.
What is an amphibian after all
but a creature that cannot quite make up its mind?
I also am of two minds, or rather many minds,
because humans have been all of these things
before we became what we are.
And what exactly are we then?
And what exactly are we becoming?

Dead Snapping Turtle

I brake for the living,
not often for the dead,
but I'll always make an exception
for a snapping turtle.
This one was on Route 131 as I was
heading north from my workplace.
As soon as I saw her
I pulled off the road
just ahead of where she lay
in the breakdown lane,
first to make sure
she was out of pain, and second
to give her the respect
that the driver who killed her did not.
I say "her" because the female snapper
has shorter nails than the male.
The last male she met had left her
with a bellyful of eggs
conceived in the honeymoon suite
of the swamp and needing now
to be laid in dryer, sandier soil.
The last mistake she made
was trying to cross the highway
from east to west without
birdwings or fleet mammal feet.
Biting is the only thing
a snapping turtle does quickly.
She might have been clipped by a truck
carrying milk for America's young,
or perhaps a compact car driven
by a woman on her way
to meet with her obstetrician.
The turtle's sharp-ridged shell was riven
in two places, her neck broken,
her eight-pointed star eyes open in death
and already the flies were using her
for their personal hatchery.
No matter what death does
everything else in this world
is frantically trying to get born.

I picked her up by the tail
and carried her to the other side
of the road, that much closer
to her goal, where I laid her
in the grass beyond the gravel,
a makeshift graveyard gift
from a distant human cousin
hurrying home.

Starlings Eating Frozen Pizza

The pizza has been wrestled half out of its red cardboard
box by a small flock of them at the side of an intersection
on an overpass. Did it fall off of a delivery bicycle?
Unlikely when it's ten below zero. It must have
been thrown or dropped here through a car window
and now it's anybody's pie, even these garbage birds,
members of an invasive brown species that has only
been here a century and a half, still resented by nativists
as if there's a Daughters of the American Revolution
for birds. The real reason they provoke anger is that
they haven't had the good taste to die, they compete
quite effectively with each other and everyone else.
They slash at the pizza and occasionally their neighbors
with a technique called open-bill probing, stabbing
and then forcing the bill a bit wider. What works
for getting grubs in bark also doubles as nature's
makeshift pizza cutter, and in no time at all the solid ice
pepperoni-and-cheese has disappeared as if this were
a college dormitory, the starlings chattering throughout.
The driver behind me lays on his horn, reminding me
that the light is green and that the starling's language
incorporates ambient noises like car horns and even
human speech. As I step on the gas the starlings scatter
upward to regroup on the power line, suddenly sedate
and well-behaved, almost assimilated.

World Records

The loudest bird call ever recorded was made
by a male white bellbird, whose mating cry
can reach 125 decibels even when the female
is already right next to him, a phenomenon
previously observed only at office Christmas parties.
The former record holder was the screaming piha
at 116 decibels. (Note to self: remember
to rename my punk group the Screaming Pihas.)
I prefer quieter birds myself, like the turkey vulture
who's been circling me for three days,
looking for any sign of weakness, his shadow
crisscrossing my deck again and again.
About his personal life I know nothing,
but I can tell you what he wants for dinner.
And honestly, he's welcome to nibble on my carcass
as long as he doesn't start until sometime after death.
Just now I am in the process of perfecting my own mating cry,
a kind of refined whimper that ends with a sob
and goes well with a glass of red wine sipped in solitude.
My cry cannot begin to compete with the screaming piha,
let alone the white bellbird, and is mercifully
inaudible to human females even when they are already
right next to me. Clearly, I and my kind
are not long for this world,
and as the turkey vulture's patient shadow reminds me,
Darwin's great work must go on.

Dehydrated Tree Frog

Half-brown, half-green, half-grown and half-alive now, he must have
found his way, or lost his way, into the apartment garage,
a smooth pond of concrete into which he could not dive.
There are a few things to eat here if he could overpower them,
but nothing to drink or bathe in, and this miniscule creature
was made to live where the water meets the land,
halfway between us and the fishes.
(Maybe he's a she. How would I know?)
It can't have been more than an hour or two since his deadly mistake,
and already he's dusty, slow and shriveling,
unable to evade my hand. In most parts of the globe
the humans would consider him a delicacy.
Here he is simply a fellow traveler in need of help.
I cradle him in my palm and tip him gently
into the car's drink cozy. At the bottom of the winding drive
I stop, step to the curb, and pour him into the dewy grass,
there being no other moisture nearby, and him so close to gone.
I don't stay to watch the result, preferring to hope for the best
for this profligate, persistent, perversely persevering thing called life.

Flattened

Coming out of the breakfast restaurant and heading toward my car
I step over what I think is an autumn leaf,
brownish-green edged with red, and realize
it's a flattened frog floating on a still lake of asphalt.
If this were an episode of *CSI: Frogtown*
it could be determined that he made one proud leap off the curb
before being turned into an amphibian pancake
by a hit-and-run inflatable tire.
Who do I call? Who do I get in touch with?
Is there a Mrs. Frog in the marsh down the hill,
hiding among the cattails and waiting for her little man
to come home? She'll be waiting a long time.
Are there tadpoles who just became orphans?
They're America's problem now, but America has enough problems,
beset as she is on all sides by those two implacables,
death and eternity. As with almost everything that gives me pause,
there is nothing to be done, so nothing is what I do,
very carefully, looking both ways as I cross to my car.

Ode to the Poplar

Such modest ambitions, to grow only up,
not out, reaching for the sky
and sometimes getting to one-hundred-sixty-five feet
with up to an eight-foot trunk
like a giant green-and-brown snake standing on its head.
You are easy on the eyes but provide little shade,
catching Monet's attention without blocking his light,
useful for making into almost everything
from toothpicks to pallets to snowboards,
and yes, matchsticks, so that after death some of you
can return to destroy so many others
planted too close together like husbands and wives
who hated each other but already bought the burial plots.
Your cousin the cottonwood has leaves that twist and shimmer
in the sun, and so do you, each one a green reflector
blinking on and off, transfixing the eye with patterns
that constantly shift without becoming anything in particular,
yet the overall effect is of stillness in the midst of change,
and the louder their rustling, the more one can sense
a quietude at the core of you, a place
that fires and saws and leveling winds cannot touch.
All at once I am ashamed of the toothpick in my hand,
and let it fall to the ground without touching my teeth.

First Flakes

The day kept trying to dawn
and finally gave up, as if to say
today has been cancelled
due to lack of photons.
Nothing but wind and cold all
afternoon in the deepening gray
lashing us poor souls below.
At the hour of not quite twilight
the first flakes come down
slantwise like drunken
debutantes descending
a spiral staircase to
the bargain basement.
They giggle and collapse on
each other, beginning to pile up.
It may be months before we can
scrape away their costume jewelry.

Delayed Spring

Suppressed by snow, each yellow tulip
is a beautiful woman coming late to the party.
No matter when she arrives, she is welcome.

Half Gone

The world is half gone,
whited out by the dusty snow
falling lightly yet continuously
for a day and a night.
Some things are still showing:
tree trunks, stalks of grass,
green sprigs of pine needles
spreading their little fans
lower down on the tree,
two squirrel nests.
The undersides of branches
are dark openings
into another dimension.
No birds, no visible animal life.
The sky a smudge of gray
made by a dirty eraser.
All is silent, expectant,
a held breath.
A real storm is coming.
Then we shall see
what, if anything, remains.

III.

Mortal Loves, Tribes, Families

Robin

I remember how your lips tasted
on the school bus, Robin, like jam
from some unknown berry, how quickly
they parted and opened for me,
promising other openings, but also
other partings, and I
never even knew your last name.
I can still see the sun on your face
and in your wide blue eyes
that stayed open the whole time,
the ember of memory still glows,
and now it also burns, a sweet stinging
fire that never quite consumes itself.

The Argument

Impossible?

When the moon tells stories
and the olive trees believe them,
huddled, their leaves quivering.

When the wind limps from roof to roof
and tries on, briefly, a paper hat, tilted
in the green light.

Impossible?

When the feather in the paperweight
shivers, struggles to rise,
edges toward the glass . . .

When the shoes, now a little out of style,
feel an urge for the sea,
for the endless stairs of water.

Impossible. Or maybe—

when your eyes tell me,
and your precise hands, folded that way—
impossible!

Until the memory of things once possible
is like a candle we burn for someone
buried alive.

Story

A man is wounded by lightning.
He gets up, smoke still rising from his rags.
He takes a step, and another . . .
This goes on for a while.
But once touched that way,
how difficult, suddenly, to imagine
the life ahead.
What days or years could tip the scales
against such a moment?
What hand could stand the comparison?
The wound never closes;
it grows like the grin of an imbecile, and the man
sickens and dies.
The wound, however, has found a reason to live,
going about the man's business
in his shoes, in his rags.

What's-Her-Face

They locked me in a dark room
with what's-her-face
to see which of us would emerge alive.
"Imperishable!" I hissed.
She recoiled while the word
went off to slit its wrists.
"Taxable income!" she retorted.
I was stunned, caught off guard.
I began to feel about the size of a voodoo doll.
"Total commitment!" I threw at her,
but it might as well have been a marshmallow.
"Arctic . . . funereal . . ." I was desperate
and she knew it. She paused for several years
to apply some eyeliner.
Her last words to me were: "Executive whole life."
They didn't hurt, didn't kill,
but they brought the house down
with a frail rain of sawdust.

The Sound of Weeping

The sound of weeping woke me in the night;
It was you, half-sleeping and half-awake,
Who cut the silence with a cry so white
With grief that all not broken had to break;
My heart broke with your heart, the dark dissolved
Into broken sobs caught in one white throat,
And for a moment everything devolved
On a single mournful perishing note.
Long ago I heard a loon cry, far off,
Inconsolable on the wide waters
While thunder, murmuring, stifled a cough
And rain made music in smothered gutters.
Why it wept—for what, or who—I never
Knew, though I carry that bird forever.

Still

There is the stillness of rot,
mold slowly, quietly overrunning and reclaiming
the fruit.
This is not that.
The stillness of fear, of children huddled in the closet
without breathing,
hiding from the drunken father.
Nor that either.
And the stillness of death, in which only the beards
and fingernails of the departed
can grow.
No.
This is something completely
other, a stillness that engenders
the more we are entangled and unable
to tell where one leaves off and the other
begins,
making sounds we can't even hear ourselves
no longer aware of ourselves,
a stillness more pronounced for being
anything but silent.
The stillness of wonder that such a moment
can still be in a world of
rot and fear and death.
When we were younger this might have led
to a baby, but that was long ago
in another life.
Still we are making something new
between us, two into one,
blue eyes and brown,
me into you,
hands cradling faces
like rivers searching for an ocean
without a shore.

Looking into a Face

Symmetrical?
Not exactly.
"There is no excellent beauty without
some strangeness in the proportion,"
said Francis Bacon,
which beats to hell anything
I could come up with.
He was probably looking in the mirror
when that line came to him
and I like to think maybe
he cut himself shaving, but I'm looking
at you,
into a face I love.
While I could happily praise your eyes, gazing into me
and beyond,
it would have to be
one at a time,
they are so different.
Meanwhile we are somewhat preoccupied
with me in you
and you under and around me and time
coming to a halt as it does
every time,
our faces so different
from each other and even from
twin parts of themselves, yet the parts
are beautiful
and the whole cannot begin to be sung.
We prefer a broken symmetry,
who knows why,
like the one they say
began the universe,
matter and antimatter annihilating each other
at ever so slightly different rates
and the tiny extra bit of matter left over
making everything that was and is and will be,
you and me,
faces and eyes,
bodies into bodies, broken
but beautiful,
world without end.

The Artist in Her Garden

This too a palette bringing forth beauty:
from chaos, order; from dark earth, color.
Now browns, blacks, whites and grays
erupt into spring like a madwoman
with a box of crayons marking the asylum walls,
except that these blossoms calm the heart
as they dazzle the eye.
There is peace in this profusion,
a quiet center, which is the fire pit
ringed by rough wooden benches and rusted iron.
The pit holds only last year's ashes,
the benches seat only ghosts
and the laughter of ghosts.
But soon there will come new fire,
new laughter, new love, or rather
old love made new by an almost imperceptible
tilting of the turning earth beneath the sun,
older than time yet evergreen.
The picture pleases, though it cannot
be framed and hung over the mantle.

Elemental

A sylph with auburn hair
and green eyes that gaze
right through you,
missing nothing, weighing everything,
you hope to find favor
with this spirit of the air
as she is drawn to the things of earth,
digging in the dirt,
planting flowers, only some of which
will bloom in her lifetime.
What does she seek down there?
Is she looking for her soul?
But she's found it
you want to tell her,
making love in the secret garden
of her sheets, learning how strong
two small thighs can be,
pale clouds full of rain
that must be released,
and somewhere very near yet unseen
something is singing,
a song of sky and grass,
the sweet piercing cry
of the bird that is her.

On Losing Again

The sun came up and, overcome with disgust,
went back down again immediately.
On the other side of the sky the quarter-moon
paused, uncertain of what to do next.
The rest of us went about our business,
preparing to make widgets,
sell widgets, buy widgets,
or to kill or be killed by the enemy,
as if those were all separate and distinct things.
That sound cutting through you could be
the shrieking of seagulls, a factory whistle
or a mad trumpet urging the troops
to a final, desperate charge.
Death is pulling a double shift
this morning, if it is morning.
Nobody gets a day off anymore.
The only time left is overtime.
History is written by the winners,
which means we will no longer be writing ours.
The end of an empire can be as edifying
as the beginning, there is still so much
to learn if there is anyone left
a couple of centuries from now to learn it.
I can hardly wait.
Meanwhile I am on death's crew,
and I intend to earn my pay
by the light of the sun or the moon
or the bomb that keeps going off in my head.

Conspiracy Theories

I suspect the woodpecker
knows Morse code
and the groundhog is concealing
explosives in his burrow.

Two clouds were seen
colluding to the point
that now there
is only one.

The sun pretended to go
down then snuck back up
to snap our pictures
with an infrared camera.

And those angels dancing
on the head of a pin?
Well, they're no angels
and that's not dancing.

Entropy

Scientists call it the measure of the disorder
or randomness in a system.
Too abstract?
Then reduce it to this: it's hard,
very hard, to make things better
but it's always possible to make them worse.
Thus relationships, children, companies, countries.
Entropy is the clock that forever
runs forward and down until it no longer
resembles a clock at all.
Meanwhile the love leaks out of marriages
one molecule at a time,
airlines beat passengers in their seats
and drag them screaming off the plane,
and on our enemies we drop bombs so big
they dwarf our own disorder, or so
we think, or would think, if thinking were something
still within our grasp.
I must make time in my desert of a day
to visit the grave of Robinson Jeffers and tell
his silent stone that our republic
no longer shines as it perishes
and entropy is the reason.
I'm sure that will comfort his departed shade,
long since dissipated into millions of strange shadows
by that other, more efficient entropy, death.

"Today I am occupied . . ."

Today I am occupied by the corpses
of the newly dead,
they pour in from the screens
of my laptop and television,
they leap through my eyes
and into my head from newspapers lying
on shelves at the convenience store,
they settle straight to my feet
and it seems there's always room
for more, I am not overflowing
and they weigh nothing.
My heart can take it.
My heart which can take marriage
and divorce and an American
hamburger with a fried egg on it.
My soul, on the other hand. . .
my soul, my soul is lost
among so many others
falling like snow,
the silence an ink blot
spreading on a tablecloth
claiming the white for its own.

Forbidden Thoughts

You'd better take them to the grave, those thoughts
That run counter to preferred narratives.
Life now is a series of *musts* and *oughts*.
Everybody who's alive today lives
In terror of being canceled or doxed
Or fired or sued or assassinated.
The witch hunters can never be outfoxed.
Where you were loved they will make you hated
And burn your miserable life to the ground.
It makes no difference at all what is true,
What extenuating facts can be found.
Speak your whole mind and you will surely rue
The day you mentioned those things forbidden.
If you have such thoughts, best keep them hidden.

Negatives

What isn't said
speaks more loudly.
What doesn't exist
bedazzles and bedevils what does.
What's left undone
keeps happening anyway to everyone I love.
Sleep does not come
or it comes too easily.
No matter.
There is no comfort here,
no place of peace or healing.
In the country of the blind
the one-eyed man is a pickpocket
silently lifting the few things
we thought still belonged to us,
leaving us disillusioned
but slightly better informed.

Déjà Vu

If you live long enough, you get to watch the wheel turn
back to the beginning, you see the cycles repeat,
never exactly, but close enough for déjà vu to leave you
wide-eyed in that vast empty desert between laughing and crying.

Twice now I have watched my nation lose its mind
and descend into hateful chaos and confusion.
The first time there was a war—just the one, how quaint!—
but that was enough back then—
and an agonizing division between generations and races.
People marched and screamed, for and against, against and for,
it didn't seem to matter which,
the main thing was to be marching and screaming.
Cities burned, people died, cops and protesters, along with a few
innocents unlucky or foolish enough to be caught between them.
One thing about those burnings years ago: I don't recall
mayors and governors and district attorneys handing out the matches.
After the sounds of bullets and bombs had died down,
after the sirens and flames and ghostly wails had dribbled into silence,
we had added to the sum total of human happiness and understanding
several small piles of ashes that could no longer be identified.
In the end, the president almost everyone had come to despise,
the one hounded from office rightfully or wrongfully,
was the one who actually stopped the war he hadn't started,
and ever since, the haters who thought they were lovers
have taken all the credit.

As suddenly as the madness had come upon us the fever broke,
we shook ourselves like babies and returned to our usual state
of semi-consciousness, blessedly unable to remember
what had just happened, once again innocent of all our crimes
and thus leaving a bullet in the chamber
for the next time, this time, which has a charm all its own,
mixing manmade disaster with natural disease.
Up is down, right is wrong, hate is love, war is peace,
but black is most definitely not white.
That one we seem to have sorted out a little.
The wheel turns, we are all bound to it,
and if you are wondering where it will stop
you don't know the nature of wheels, or the wheel of nature.

Focus Group

Would you like to join our focus group?
Our corporate sponsor prefers to remain anonymous,
Though you'd recognize their name if you were a blood spatter expert
With knowledge of ancient Sumerian death rituals.

They hope to learn how long a man
Can scream under water before he realizes no help is coming
And that whatever is about to devour him will soon be
Swallowed whole by something even bigger.

Would you like to take part? This prestige research project
Is sure to change the way we look at the soul
As it separates from the mortified flesh like a puffball mushroom
Exploding at midnight in the forest.

Our focus group needs you, and you, and you, if only
Because the digging will go so much faster, and the placing of stones,
And the numbering of atrocities will add up to so much more
Than the square root of a charred and paralytic zero.

The Germ of an Idea

The world as we know
it is full of bacteria,
like the kind that crowds between lips
to keep the word "love" from entering or escaping,
or the kind that eats our meals
and digests them for us,
or the kind we elect to the presidency,
after which we must invent vaccines
to protect the innocent, who are also
a form of bacteria,
mostly innocuous;
even our literature,
which will soon become infested with this theme,
is written of the bacteria, by the bacteria
and for the bacteria,
who shall not perish from the earth,
as witness the gentle billions of bacilli that
have grouped themselves selflessly together
to form the letters of this
letter to them.

Mindfulness

I practice a very special
form of mindfulness
called not-minding-ness.
This has brought me peace and purified
my soul to the point that it is almost
possible to live with me.
My sacred principles are:
Read no newspapers.
Watch no television.
Stay the hell offline.
Do not discuss religion or politics
with anyone dumber than yourself
or smarter than yourself
for in neither instance
will there be enlightenment.
Remain silent at all costs
unless you are being tortured nonstop
in which case it is acceptable
to scream occasionally.
If a spider is crawling over you
let him crawl;
he may well be more evolved
and he comes by his poison honestly.
Above everything be still
and know that this world
means to kill us all
and will eventually succeed.
Relax. The worst has already happened.

The Dream

Five years old, I dream
of the dark and a terrible dance.
Amid gravel and driven dust
squats a town of wretched little pueblos,
no more than walls, really, open to the sky.
There the townspeople move as one, spasmodic,
soundless in their circling.
As my eyes grow accustomed to the night
I see they are joined in a crooked line
by a length of crooked
pipe welded to their heads.
I'm afraid; I run; they follow and catch me.
They fuse me to the pipe and I stop struggling.
Suddenly I'm one of them;
I can appreciate their point of view.
I see they are beautiful
and the dance meaningful.

Family Metaphors

Our household was a novel inside a play,
the novel being *Lord of the Flies*
and the play being *Who's Afraid of Virginia Woolf?*
Seven feral children shipwrecked on the reef of a bad marriage
made a savage society of their own devices,
a tribe doomed to wander the deserted suburban island
on which they found themselves stranded.
Their double sentence: life without parole, death by madness.
Seven bodies survived, seven sarcophagi
filled with psyches crushed to dust.
Did you know that in the netherworld the dead eat their own,
there being nothing else? And then they are all
eaten by sand and waves and wind and time.
It's another story without a happy ending,
a story with the single lonely virtue of being true.

Home

Home is where the telltale heart is, beating
Beneath the floorboards and driving us mad.
The sins of the fathers bear repeating
In families, whether happy or sad
Or simply too tired to resist the pull
Of intergenerational decay.
Drink deeply of despair. Your glass is full
And will remain so every night and day
That you try to survive under this roof,
A shadow among shadows, a gray ghost
Whose mere existence provides ample proof
That some things take a long time to be lost.
Enter the home, you will enter the heart.
And then tear it, tear it, tear it apart.

Gertrude

Our father brought you home from a fossil-hunting trip
on the bluffs above the Rock River,
where his Marine Corps buddy Rick
may have saved his life by commanding him
to pause over your coiled form in mid-step.
We expected them to bring back a box of ancient stones,
not a living fossil with the power to kill in its fangs,
but the most disturbing part was how easily
a timber rattler became a member of our family,
how well you fit in with the cats, dogs,
geese, chickens and turtles, not to mention
one white mouse named Melvin
and the crow we called Edgar Allan Crow.
Not that we allowed you to mingle—
especially not with Melvin. You spent your days
in the crawlspace (how apropos)
in a box of wood and glass, watching and waiting.
When the neighbor children got out of hand
we would bring them to you and rap on your box
until you struck. The venom dribbling down
the inside of the glass was more eloquent
than anything we could have said.
After a time our parents tired of the novelty
and donated you to the Brookfield Zoo, where you
were killed by a falling rock six months later.
We never believed it was an accident.
I think of you now as the perfect metaphor
for our home: in the whitewashed house at the end
of a gravel road that presented a bright façade
to the world, you were a dose of death and poison
lurking beneath the floorboards, unsleeping,
the author of my lifelong insomnia, the one
who taught me to look on life with rattlesnake eyes.

Willow

Towering over my childhood
in the backyard was a weeping willow,
and let me tell you
we gave her plenty to cry about,
grinning skulls carved into her flesh
with tenpenny nails, and later
a highwire contraption cutting deep into her trunk
on which we could hang-slide between
the tree and a telephone pole,
a two-way trip to nowhere
always ending with a slam into hardwood
except when we fell off first
and slammed into stony earth instead,
somewhat dangerous but
excellent preparation for life. Other things
the willow witnessed without comment
would have brought the authorities,
if there were any who cared,
to take our parents away in handcuffs
and parcel us out to foster homes.
Yet in this too her silent sobs
were a kind of lesson
about helplessness
and the uselessness of roots.

A Shock of Recognition

Once I saw a fisherman
who had caught a turtle instead of a fish,
a giant snapping turtle he laid on its craggy back
and stabbed through the neck with a hand-carved wooden spear,
leaving it half-alive but helpless.
It couldn't turn over, couldn't walk away,
couldn't even bite anything anymore,
only writhe and hiss and tread the air in mute agony,
and I whispered to myself as I passed
my twin, my brother.

Baked

There are worse ways to enter the workforce
than by washing dishes in a bakery.
After cleaning a hundred angel food cake pans in a day,
doing the dishes at home will never again
feel like a chore. Piece of cake!

Once or twice an hour the counter girls
would step from the shop into the back room
to have a cigarette and bare their breasts at us
by the dim red light of the ovens,
as if unveiling two more fresh loaves.

This was back when employee morale
used to mean something.
Certainly it caused me to scrub more furiously.
Cyd was in love with me but I was in love
with Jennie, a triangle no geometry could ever resolve.

Those of us in the back would also sometimes
pause to peer through the blinds at the parade of humanity
in the shop, including local celebrities like the mayor
and Ringmaster Ned from *Bozo's Circus*
who needed his prune kolaches every Friday.

Mr. Belushi came by several times a week
but no one knew who his sons were yet,
so to us he was just another crazy Albanian.
The real fun began every evening after the shop closed
and the Pennsylvania Dutch couple who owned the place

climbed upstairs to their second-floor apartment.
The rest of us would share a joint
lit in the glow of the ovens and have food fights
with handfuls of whipped cream
and lard scooped out of giant tubs.

Afterward we would carefully put everything
back in its place, because waste is a sin.
I was not able to eat baked goods for the next decade,
and to this day the smell of warm bread
arouses me in a way I can't begin to explain.

The Music of the Words

Our mother would recite Yeats,
Frost, Dylan Thomas and Shakespeare
while doing housework or cooking,
she was a terrible housekeeper
and her cooking was one step removed
from negligent homicide,
but she had a lovely voice
which made the words sing
with a hey nonny nonny
and a permanent case
of postpartum depression.
Sometimes she switched to ballads
made popular among American folkies
by the Clancy Brothers,
Pete Seeger and Joan Baez.
Either way the music of the words
sunk in deep, the difference between
conversation and verse
was not lost in translation,
the rhythms and rhymes
made it all stick
and we learned that poetry
is simply part of life
like sweeping the floor badly
or burning the toast in tune.

Baby's First Lie

She slaps in anger,
wanting or not wanting something—
who knows what?—
and then seeing her mother's look
feigns gentleness, the slap becoming
a friendly pat,
but the eyes still impudent
and a crooked smile forming
in spite of herself.
And all this before the first word.

I'm Ready

Not that I'm looking to go
any time soon, mind you,
but if death should take me now
I would not feel cheated.
I've tasted everything this life
can offer: love, true and false,
hate, always true (why is it
hate that's always true?),
the quarter moon a slice of blood orange
just above the horizon,
the sun at twilight a tulip dipped in lava,
the music of Bach
which by itself justifies
all the failings of humanity,
the bittersweet joy of fatherhood—
helping a soul to grow
even as she grows away from you . . .
Yes, I've seen it all:
two giant snapping turtles making love
very carefully, as they say,
a redwood tree that wears a cloud
for a hat,
a Dutch still life
more beautiful than any real fruit,
and a heart that beats only for me
day and night.
Whatever the foreshortened future may hold
it can't surpass any of these,
so to echo my beloved Bach,
"Come, sweetest death."
I'm ready.
Just not quite yet,
if it's all the same to you.
I want to spend some time
with that beating heart.

❋

Acknowledgements

Grateful acknowledgment is made to the following publications and their editors for first publishing many of the poems collected here, sometimes in different versions:

The American Journal of Poetry: "Socrates"

Antiphon: "Where Do We Come From? What Are We? Where Are We Going?"

Atticus Review: "Conspiracy Theories"

Bacopa Literary Review: "The Music of the Words"

The Big Windows Review: "Today I am occupied . . ."

Bracken: "Dead Snapping Turtle"

Burningword Literary Journal: "Entropy"

Crosswinds Poetry Journal: "The Argument," "First Flakes"

Die Leere Mitte: "Family Metaphors"

Doubly Mad Journal: "Apology," "Mine"

Exacting Clam: "Déjà Vu," "Elemental," "Forbidden Thoughts"

The Fieldstone Review: "Do You Know These 10 Common Warning Signs of Depression?"

Former People Journal: "Looking into a Face," "The Germ of an Idea," "Focus Group"

Grey Sparrow Journal (Snow Jewel 7): "Spider"

Hawaii Pacific Review: "A Real Question with No Real Answers"

The Hollins Critic: "First and Last"

Into the Void: "I long to enter the unholy. . ."

JMWW: "Sudden Silence"

Light: "Psalm"

London Grip: "The Two Lights"

Lothlorien Poetry Journal: "Baby's First Lie," "Tabula Rasa," "Robin," "Nonbeing"

The MacGuffin: "Around the Block"

MacQueen's Quinterly: "Coffee"

Minetta Review: "Homunculus"

MockingHeart Review: "Dehydrated Tree Frog"

Noctua Review: "The Sound of Weeping"

The Nonconformist: "A Mist in the Tree," "Secret Messages"

The Ocotillo Review: "A Shock of Recognition"

The Opiate: "Flattened," "Baked"

Otis Nebula: "What's-Her-Face," "Story," "Meditation"

Quail Bell Magazine: "Two Sisters"

Rathalla Review: "A Song of Starlight"

Rattle Poetry: "All of My Fathers"

Roanoke Review: "A Last Villanelle"

Sand Hills Literary Magazine: "On Losing Again," "The Rains of October"

Sheila-Na-Gig: "Still," "Fog and Fire"

South Florida Poetry Journal: "Listening to Arvo Pärt's *Tabula Rasa*," "The Dog One Floor Up," "Starlings Eating Frozen Pizza"

Steam Ticket: "World Records"

The Sun Magazine: "Mindfulness," "False Spring"

Two Thirds North: "I'm Ready"

Verse-Virtual: "The Dream"

The Whiskey Blot: "Tree," "A Brief Word About the Moon"

Wilderness House Literary Review: "Encounter"

Willawaw Journal: "Ode to the Poplar," "No Reason"

The poem "My Dream" was originally published in the chapbook *The Sound of One Hand Slapping* (SurVision Books).

The following poems are being published here for the first time: "The Artist in Her Garden," "Breakfast with Death," "Coyote," "Death Row," "Delayed Spring," "Gertrude," "Half Gone," "Home," "Negatives," "Ode to Silence," "Ode to the Swamp."

I wish to offer a special thank you to my publisher Jacob Smullyan of Sagging Meniscus Press and Exacting Clam for giving my work such a fine home.

Photo credit: Scott Erskine

Kurt Luchs was born in Cheektowaga, New York, grew up in Wheaton, Illinois, and has lived and worked all over the United States, mostly in publishing and media. Currently he's based in Kalamazoo, Michigan. His first poetry publication came at age 16 in the long-gone journal *Epos*, right next to a poem by Bukowski. He has also written comedy for television (*Politically Incorrect* with Bill Maher and the *Late Late Show* with Craig Kilborn) and radio (American Comedy Network), as well as contributing humor to the *New Yorker*, the *Onion* and *McSweeney's Internet Tendency*, among others. In addition to the current volume, Sagging Meniscus Press published his first full-length poetry collection, *Falling in the Direction of Up* (2021), and the humor collection *It's Funny Until Someone Loses an Eye (Then It's Really Funny)* (2017). His poetry chapbooks include *One of These Things Is Not Like the Other* (Finishing Line Press 2019), and *The Sound of One Hand Slapping* (SurVision Press 2022). He won a 2022 Pushcart Prize, a 2021 James Tate Poetry Prize, the 2021 Eyelands Book Award for Short Stories, and the 2019 *Atlanta Review* International Poetry Contest. He is a Contributing Editor of *Exacting Clam*, the literary journal from Sagging Meniscus.

www.ingramcontent.com/pod-product-compliance
Lightning Source LLC
Chambersburg PA
CBHW020211090426
42734CB00008B/1020